S0-AAD-788

Astronomy

Philip Steele

CRESTWOOD HOUSE
New York

What is astronomy?

From the earliest times, humans have been fascinated by the Sun and Moon, and the stars and planets. It took scientists many hundreds of years to begin to understand how the planets and stars move through space. They invented telescopes to map the night sky. They also invented equipment to send into space itself to study the planets and stars. The scientific study of space and all it contains is called astronomy.

The first stargazers

Long ago, people worshiped the Sun and the Moon. Priests realized that they needed to study the sky in order to work out the best time to sow crops. Stonehenge (right) may have been used for studying the angle of the sunrise about 4,000 years ago. Circles of stone still stand in southern England.

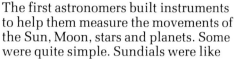

Mapping the stars

The first astronomers built instruments to help them measure the movements of the Sun, Moon, stars and planets. Some were quite simple. Sundials were like early clocks. They used the Sun's shadow to point to the time of day. The ancient Greeks and the Arabs were expert star-gazers. They invented more complicated instruments such as the astrolabe (left). This was used to measure the exact position of the Sun and the stars in the sky.

Most early astronomers had no idea that the world was round or that it was spinning through space. They thought that it was a flat platform fixed inside a glass ball. They thought that the stars and planets moved around on this ball.

The first telescopes

When more astronomers studied the sky, some realized that they must have been wrong. In 1543 a book was published by a Polish astronomer named Copernicus. He said that the Earth traveled around the Sun.

In 1608 the telescope was invented by a Dutch eyeglass-maker named Hans Lippershey. Some of the best telescopes were made by an Italian astronomer named Galileo Galilei (left). He used them to study the sky and proved that Copernicus was right.

3

How do telescopes work?

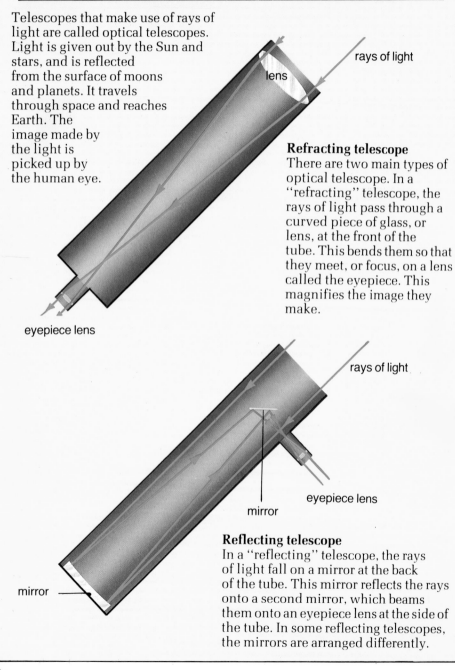

Telescopes that make use of rays of light are called optical telescopes. Light is given out by the Sun and stars, and is reflected from the surface of moons and planets. It travels through space and reaches Earth. The image made by the light is picked up by the human eye.

rays of light

lens

eyepiece lens

Refracting telescope
There are two main types of optical telescope. In a "refracting" telescope, the rays of light pass through a curved piece of glass, or lens, at the front of the tube. This bends them so that they meet, or focus, on a lens called the eyepiece. This magnifies the image they make.

rays of light

mirror

eyepiece lens

mirror

Reflecting telescope
In a "reflecting" telescope, the rays of light fall on a mirror at the back of the tube. This mirror reflects the rays onto a second mirror, which beams them onto an eyepiece lens at the side of the tube. In some reflecting telescopes, the mirrors are arranged differently.

Giant telescopes

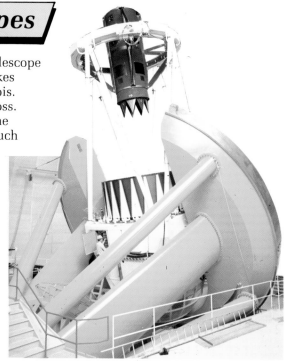

The world's biggest refracting telescope was built in 1897. It is at the Yerkes Observatory, near Chicago, Illinois. It has a lens that is 40 inches across. Today's giant telescopes are of the reflecting type. Mirrors give a much clearer image. The whole telescope is controlled by computers. Instead of looking at the image through an eyepiece, modern astronomers use electronic equipment that reacts to light. Photographs are taken of the image. Some of the telescopes in use today are huge. A human figure is dwarfed by the biggest telescope at the Kitt Peak Observatory in Arizona (right). It has a mirror that is 157 inches across.

Telescopes in space

The air, heat and dust around our planet make it hard to obtain a clear image through a telescope. The glare of city lights can also spoil the view. For this reason, big telescopes are often sited far from towns, on mountaintops. There the layer of air is thinner. In recent years telescopes have been carried into space itself on board spacecraft. In space there is no air at all and telescopes can obtain very clear images. Photographs taken in space can be sent back to Earth as radio signals or carried back by astronauts. The Hubble Space Telescope, launched in 1990 (left), circles the Earth. It is able to see stars and planets 100 times more clearly than telescopes on Earth can.

What are radio telescopes?

Objects in space do not only give off light rays. They also give off radio waves, X rays, ultraviolet and infrared rays. Light and these other rays travel through space with a wave motion. The distance between dips or crests is called the wavelength. Radio waves have longer wavelengths than the other rays. They can be picked up by radio telescopes (left). The dish picks up radio waves and reflects them onto a central antenna. The waves are then turned into electrical signals.

X-ray detectors

Light and radio waves can pass through the air, or atmosphere, that surrounds our planet. X rays, which have short wavelengths, cannot. This is why X-ray detectors must be at least 90 miles above the Earth. The first ones were sent up on balloons or rockets. Today X-ray detectors pick up X rays coming from distant stars. The signals sent back are turned into pictures (right) by computers.

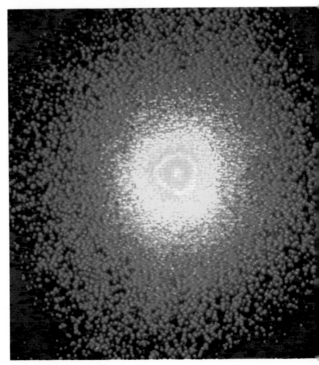

What are ultraviolet telescopes?

Stars, especially new and very large ones, give off large amounts of ultraviolet rays. These have a shorter wavelength than light rays, and only a few pass through the atmosphere. The best place to pick up ultraviolet rays is out in space. The International Ultraviolet Explorer (left) was launched in 1978. It was equipped with a special telescope fitted with instruments called spectrometers. The signals sent back were turned into fascinating pictures of distant stars.

What are infrared telescopes?

[In]frared rays have a longer [w]avelength than light rays do. They [a]re given out by hot objects in space. [W]hen you feel the heat of the Sun, [yo]u are feeling infrared rays that [ha]ve traveled 90 million miles [to] Earth. Infrared rays can pass [thr]ough the Earth's atmosphere. [Sp]ecial telescopes have been built to [de]tect them on Earth. They are sited [on] mountain peaks, where they [are] less affected by water vapor [an]d other gases that absorb [the] rays. Infrared detectors [ma]y also be carried up on [air]craft or balloons. The best [pl]ace for infrared telescopes [is i]n space. The InfraRed [As]tronomy Satellite (IRAS) [(ri]ght) was launched in 1983.

Looking at the northern sky

When we look at the night sky, we see the light rays given off by millions of stars. Each of these is a distant sun. The stars seem to make patterns, called constellations, in the sky. Long ago the constellations were named in the Latin language after animals, objects or people. Which constellations we see depends upon where we are standing on Earth. Below is a map of the sky as it is seen in northern parts of the world. Look for Ursa Minor and Ursa Major. The star Polaris can be seen above the North Pole.

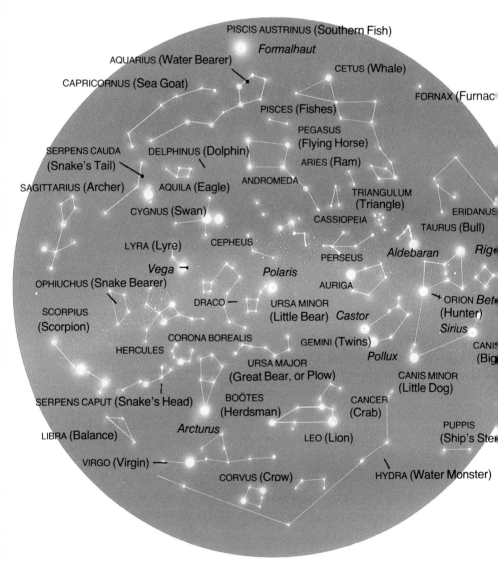

Looking at the southern sky

ne easiest constellation to find in southern parts of the world is Crux. It
shaped like a cross pointing to the South Pole. Look also for Carina. The
ap below shows the southern constellations. Note that the constellations on
e edge of the map can be seen in both northern and southern lands. You do
t need a huge telescope or a special observatory to become a stargazer. On a
ear, dark night you can see about 2,000 stars with the naked eye. Binoculars
a simple telescope will help you to see thousands more.

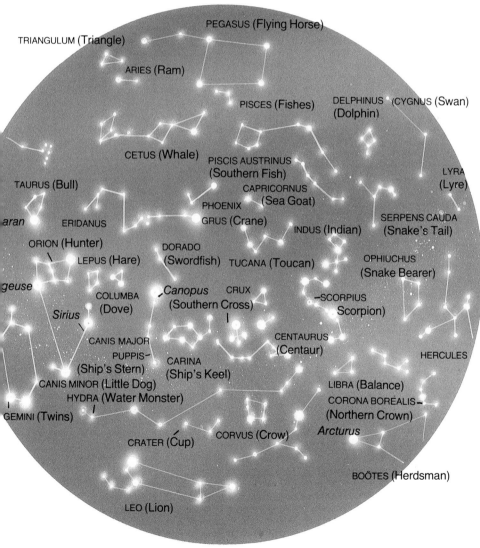

What is the Sun?

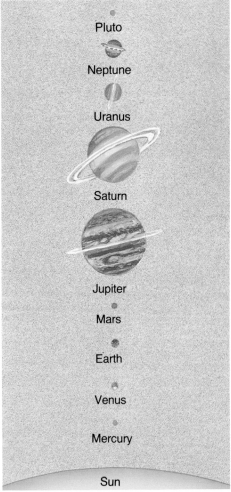

Pluto

Neptune

Uranus

Saturn

Jupiter

Mars

Earth

Venus

Mercury

Sun

The nearest star to the Earth is called the Sun. Our planet takes a year to circle, or orbit, the Sun. The Earth spins around once every 24 hours. The side facing the Sun has daylight. The other side has night. The Sun is a huge ball of gases, spinning in space. At its center, the gas hydrogen is turned into helium. Light and heat are given out in great bursts of energy. Huge tongues of hot gas shoot out into space (above).

What is the Solar System?

The Earth is not the only planet to orbit the Sun. Eight other spinning planets (left) are also in orbit. The nearest is Mercury, which is only 35 million miles from the Sun. It takes 88 days to complete one orbit. The farthest is normally Pluto, which is on average 3,000 million miles from the Sun. Part of Pluto's orbit crosses that of Neptune. Pluto takes nearly 248 years to orbit the Sun. All natural objects that orbit the Sun make up the Solar System. The planets are held in orbit by the pulling power of the Sun. Force such as this is called gravity.

What is the Moon?

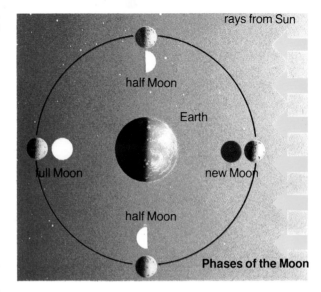

Phases of the Moon

The planet Earth has its own pulling power, or gravity. It holds a smaller world, called the Moon, in orbit around it. The Moon is 230,000 miles from Earth. It orbits once every 27 days 8 hours, almost a calendar month. In this period the Moon only spins once, so the same side always faces Earth. As the Moon orbits, different parts of it are lit up by the Sun (right). On Earth, we see only the sunlit section. We may see a full disk, a half Moon or a thin crescent. The changes in shape during each month are known as the phases of the Moon. When the orbit of the Moon passes between the Sun and the Earth, part of the Earth falls within the Moon's shadow. The Sun is eclipsed. It cannot be seen. When the Earth lies between the Sun and the Moon, the Moon is eclipsed. The gravity of the Moon is six times weaker than that of the Earth. Even so, it is strong enough to tug at the Earth's oceans, creating tides. The Moon is a world of dust and bare rock, pitted with craters.

Other Moons

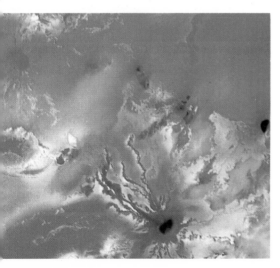

Many other planets in the Solar System have moons. Mars has two moons called Phobos and Deimos. They are chunks of rock with irregular shapes. The planet Jupiter has 16 moons. The four largest were first spotted by Galileo. Ganymede is the biggest moon in the Solar System. Like its neighbor Callisto, it is made of ice and cratered rock. Europa is smooth and icy, but the surface of Io (left) is covered with spouting volcanoes. Saturn may have as many as 23 moons. The largest, Titan, has an atmosphere. Most moons have none. Uranus has 15 moons, while Neptune has two and Pluto only one.

What are shooting stars?

Planets and moons are not the only solid objects in the Solar System. There are many tiny bits of rock flying through space. Thousands of them hit the Earth's atmosphere every day. They burn up as they fall, forming a streak of light. They are called meteors, or shooting stars. If Earth's orbit passes through a belt of these rocks, meteors fall in showers (below).

What are meteorites?

Some space rocks are very large. When they enter the Earth's atmosphere, they do not burn up. They crash into the Earth's surface. They are called meteorites. The meteorite on the right fell in Namibia, in Africa. It weighs about 60 tons. Meteorites often form craters when they crash. That is why there are so many craters on the Moon and some of the planets. On Earth most craters have been worn away by wind and rain, but some very large ones remain.

Mini-marathons

Ceres
662 miles

Pallas
365 miles

Vesta
322 miles

Juno
150 miles

Some of the rocks in the Solar System are like mini-planets (left). They are called asteroids. Asteroids are irregular lumps of rock that orbit the Sun. Most are found in a dense ring lying between the planets Mars and Jupiter. This is called the asteroid belt.

Some asteroids have orbits that pass out of this belt. Their orbits form long, looping marathons across the Solar System. Some asteroids pass close to Earth as they orbit the Sun. Others pass by the outer planets.

What are comets?

n the very edge of the
lar System, there is a
eat cloud of comets.
mets are balls of dust
d frozen gas that orbit
e Sun. Sometimes the
avity of a star beyond
e Solar System tugs at
e orbit of a comet and
shes it off course. It
ay then swing in toward
e Sun. As it approaches
e Sun, the frozen gases
at up. A long tail of gas
d dust trails across the
y (right). This can often
seen from Earth. The
met then circles the Sun
d heads back toward the
ter planets.

A closer look at the planets

The Sun and the planets were formed about 5 billion years ago from a spinning cloud of dust and gases. The dust particles stuck together to form solid planets. The planets today have centers, or cores, of rock. They may be surrounded by liquids and gases, like Jupiter's (left).

Next to the Sun

The nearest planet to the Sun is Mercury. It is hard for us to view Mercury from the Earth, because of the Sun's glare. Spacecraft have shown us an airless world of bare rock, pitted with craters (below). By night the temperature is 347° F, by day, 644° F.

The planet of love?

Venus is the easiest planet to see from Earth, because it is near and very bright. It is covered by beautiful clouds, and the Romans named it after their goddess of love. We now know that it is in fact a very harsh world. The clouds contain acid, and the atmosphere is poisonous. The surface is a desert, with an average temperature of 869° F. From Earth we can only see the part of Venus that is lighted by the Sun. Like the Moon, Venus often appears to us as a crescent. This radar map shows the shapes made by the hills and deserts of Venus.

Our home planet

Seen from the Moon (left), the planet Earth is a disk of blue and white. Its oceans are wreathed with clouds. Inside the Earth is a core of iron and layers of solid and molten rock. The water and the oxygen in the atmosphere support plant and animal life. The Sun gives the Earth light and warmth, without scorching it.

Is there life on Mars?

Mars is another planet easily seen from Earth. In some ways it is like our own planet, but so far spacecraft have not found any traces of life on it. The surface is strewn with red rocks and banked with sand dunes. Photographs of the planet have shown big volcanoes (right).

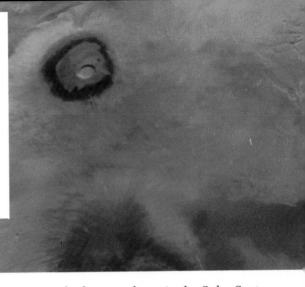

The giant planet

Jupiter is the largest planet in the Solar System. It is 11 times the size of Earth and contains 318 times as much material. Most of the planet is made the gas hydrogen in liquid form. A great red spot on the surface of Jupiter can be seen from Earth. This is thought to be a gigantic, whirling storm.

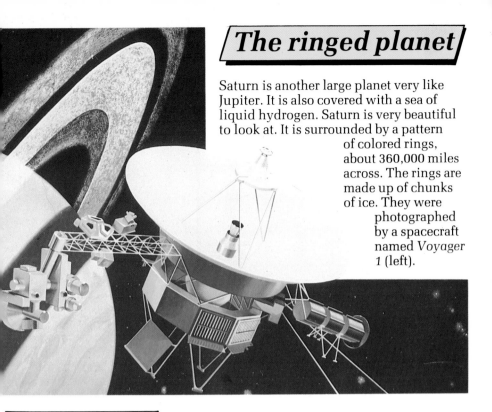

Saturn is another large planet very like Jupiter. It is also covered with a sea of liquid hydrogen. Saturn is very beautiful to look at. It is surrounded by a pattern of colored rings, about 360,000 miles across. The rings are made up of chunks of ice. They were photographed by a spacecraft named *Voyager 1* (left).

The tilted planet

Uranus can barely be seen from Earth without a telescope. The planet's surface is shrouded in a green fog. Most planets are slightly tilted as they spin. Uranus, however, lies almost on its side. Around it are rings of ice and dust (below).

The blue planet

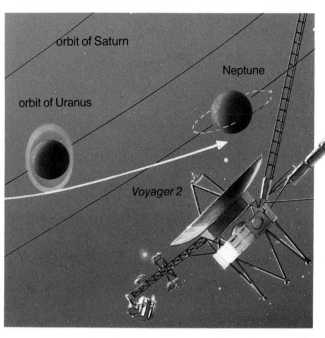

orbit of Saturn

Neptune

orbit of Uranus

Voyager 2

The picture on the left shows the spacecraft *Voyager 2* passing the orbit of the planet Neptune in 1989. The planet was unknown until 1846, and we still have much to find out about it. Both Uranus and Neptune have deep oceans of water around a rocky core. Above the blue seas of Neptune, there are white clouds of a frozen gas called methane. Astronomers think they have found an incomplete ring around Neptune. Its sections are called arcs. The orbit of the planet Pluto crosses that of Neptune. At the moment, Neptune is the farthest planet from the Sun. In 1999 Pluto will be again.

A frozen world

The planet Pluto was discovered in 1930. It is smaller than our Moon and can only be seen through large telescopes. It is probably a ball of ice and rock. The Sun is so far away from Pluto that it appears as little more than a bright star in Pluto's sky. The planet is bitterly cold and probably has no atmosphere. Pluto may once have been a moon of Neptune, which then escaped to become a planet in its own right. As it orbits the Sun, Pluto is circled by its own moon, called Charon.

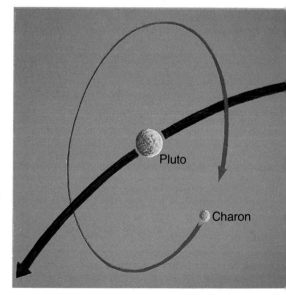

Pluto

Charon

Exploring the Solar System

ome astronomers think that there may be a tenth planet on the edge of the
olar System. This is because gravity from an unknown source, as well as from
'luto, is tugging at the orbits of Uranus and Neptune. Could this be Planet X?
t is more likely that the source of gravity, rather than being another planet, is a star
utside the Solar System.

'here are still many mysteries in the Solar System. Today astronomers have
better chance than ever of solving them. They have fine observatories and
adio telescopes on Earth, as well as telescopes and ray detectors in space.
'hey can land humans on other worlds to set up experiments. In future years
stronauts will be sent to Mars. Spacecraft without people on board, called
robes, will examine asteroids and the planet Pluto. Probes have already
rossed the Solar System, studying comets and photographing planets. *Pioneer
0* (below) was the first to leave the Solar System and head for the stars.

Big and bright stars

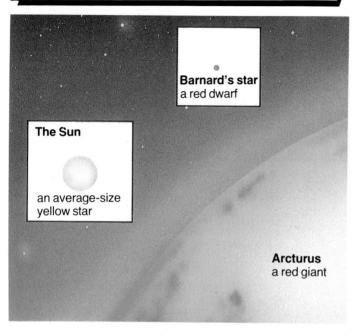

Barnard's star
a red dwarf

The Sun

an average-size
yellow star

Arcturus
a red giant

Beyond our Solar System lie countless billions of stars. Some are over 100 times bigger than our Sun. They are called supergiants. Giants are about ten times the size of the Sun. Dwarf stars may be 100 times smaller than the Sun. We can tell how hot a star is by its color. Red stars are slightly cooler than the Sun, which is yellow. Hotter stars are white or blue-white. Some stars seem bright to us on Earth. This may be because they really are bright, or because they are near to us.

Do stars last forever?

New stars are born from clouds of dust and gas spinning in space. Big stars burn up their gases in a few million years. However, a medium-size star like the Sun may last about 10 billion years. The Sun itself is halfway through its life. Before the Sun dies, it will turn into a red giant. Its gases will drift away into space. A white dwarf will be left at the center, which will slowly fade away. A big star may go out with a huge bang. Such an explosion is called a supernova. Any planets nearby would be instantly melted down (right).

What is a nebula?

Clouds of gas and dust in space are called nebulae. They are nurseries of new stars and graveyards of old stars. The Great Nebula in Orion (below) is lighted by the glow of new stars. Some nebulae block the light of stars behind them, forming dark patches.

Do other stars have planets?

When our sun was being formed in space, some of the gas and dust on the edge of the spinning cloud was not sucked into the center. It was this material that formed the planets.

It is thought that maybe one out of ten of the stars we see at night also have planets. We have not been able to see any of these planets through telescopes. However, pictures taken by the InfraRed Astronomy Satellite in 1983 seem to show planets being formed around the star Beta Pictoris (right).

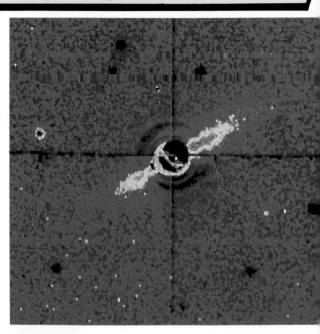

Star groupings

Many stars cling together in groups of two and threes. They are held in place by the force of gravity. Sometimes large numbers of stars are bunched together in groups called clusters. The M13 Cluster (left) appears in the constellation Hercules. It contains thousands of stars. The group is shaped like a globe and so is known as a globular cluster. Star groups that have no particular shape are called open clusters.

Astronomers measure distances in "light-years." Each light-year is the distance traveled by a ray of light in one year, which is 5.7 trillion miles. The M13 Cluster is 22,500 light-years from Earth.

1 As the bright star passes behind the faint one, the point of light we see from Earth grows faint.

bright star

faint star

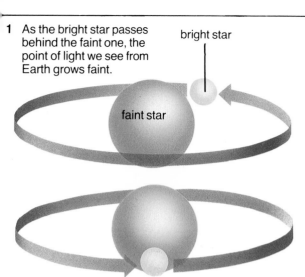

Many of the stars we see in the sky turn out to be double stars when viewed through a telescope. Some of these may simply appear to be close together when viewed from Earth. Others really are pairs, held together by gravity. They are called binaries. In a binary each star orbits the other. Sometimes one of the twins is faint and blocks the light of its brighter neighbor.

2 As the bright star passes in front of the faint one, our view of the binary grows brighter.

Stars that change size

In 1786 a single star was spotted in the constellation Cepheus, which seemed to vary its brightness. Stars such as this alter size. When they are small they are bright, and when they are big they are faint.

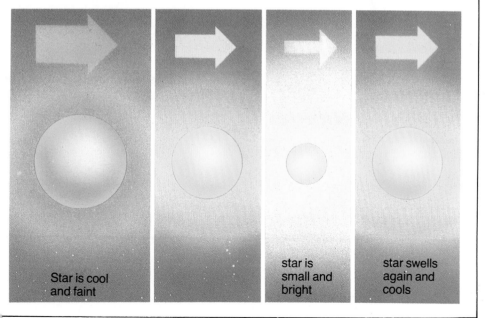

Star is cool and faint

star is small and bright

star swells again and cools

What is the Milky Way?

If you look at the night sky, you may see a hazy band of light. This is called the Milky Way, and it is made up of countless stars. Our Sun is just one star in this vast group, or galaxy. There may be over 100,000 million stars in the Milky Way galaxy (below). It is about 100,000 light-years from one side to another and 10,000 light-years thick.

What shape is our galaxy?

Viewed end on, the Milky Way galaxy is shaped like a discus. It is thicker at the center than at the edges. An overall view (right) shows the galaxy as a huge spiral, like fireworks. The arrow shows the position of our Solar System in the galaxy. The whole galaxy is moving through space. It spins once every 225 million years.

24

elliptical
galaxy
(flattened)

irregular galaxy

There may be about
100,000 million galaxies
in the whole of space, or
Universe. Most are grouped
together in clusters of
galaxies. Large galaxies
may have up to ten times
as many stars as our own.
All galaxies are spinning
as they move through
space.
Galaxies have various
shapes. Elliptical galaxies
are shaped like lemons.
Some of these are very
rounded, while others are
flattened. Irregular
galaxies have no clear
shape. They are mostly
small. Spiral galaxies
have curved arms, like
our own Milky Way
galaxy.

A barred spiral
galaxy has a
straight band of
stars across its
center, which links
curved arms.
The nearest large
galaxy to our own is
the great spiral in
the constellation of
Andromeda. It can
just be seen with the
naked eye. It is 2.2
million light-years
from Earth.
Most galaxies
seem to be about 12
billion years old.

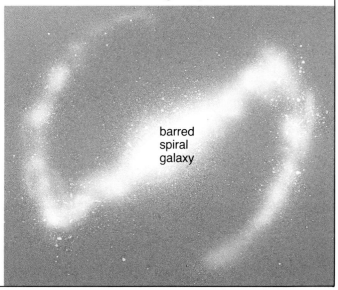

barred
spiral
galaxy

What are pulsars?

After a star has exploded, its contents may be sucked into a dense core only 12 miles across. This is made up of tiny particles called neutrons, and is known as a neutron star. Neutron stars called pulsars spin at high speed, beaming energy through space in the form of light, radio waves and sometimes X rays. The spinning motion makes them appear to flash on (below left) and off (below right).

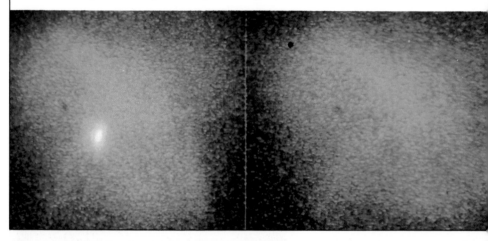

What are quasars?

The most distant sources of energy known to astronomers are called quasars. This word is short for "quasi-stellar" objects, which simply means "starlike" objects. Quasars may be only about the size of our Solar System, and yet they give out more energy than the whole of our galaxy. The X-ray picture (left) shows the first quasar to be discovered, in the Virgo galaxy cluster. Some quasars are over 10 billion light-years away, on the edge of the known Universe.

What are black holes?

The great energy given out by quasars may come from hot gases rushing into a black hole. Black holes are one of the great space puzzles. They are the remains of large stars that have exploded. The gravity at the center of a black hole becomes so strong that it sucks in surrounding gases, stars and planets (below). It even pulls back light, so that it cannot be seen with the eye. Black holes become bigger as objects are swallowed up by them. Large black holes may form the centers of galaxies.

How big is the Universe?

It is difficult for us to understand the vast distances in outer space. The way we measure things on Earth makes little sense when dealing with distant galaxies. A beam of light travels through space at 186,282 miles per second, and yet the light reaching us from some quasars started on its journey to Earth 10 billion years ago. We now know that the galaxies are moving apart from each other, and this means that the Universe must be growing all the time.

The great mystery

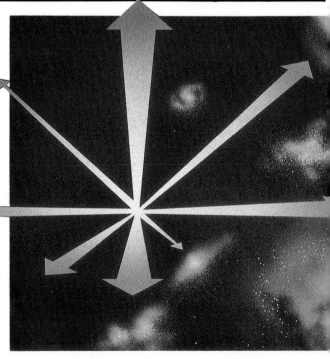

How did the Universe begin? The outward movement of the galaxies suggests that it may have started with a great explosion. Astronomers call it the "Big Bang" and think that it may have taken place about 15 billion years ago. Gases rushed outward and the galaxies were formed. Will the gravity of all the stars and planets in the Universe start to pull the Universe back together again? There might then be another Big Bang....

The challenge

A mirror 9 inches across is prepared for the Hubble Space Telescope (left). The telescope is able to trace faint objects 14 billion light-years away. It is able to see farther into deep space than any telescope ever made.

Telescopes and space probes will help us to understand how the Universe began and how it is moving. They will be able to show us planets around distant stars.

One day humans may have to leave the Earth. It may become too crowded or too polluted. Distant planets may provide new homes for people. In this way, the work being carried out by astronomers today may prove to be necessary for the future survival of the human race.

Can we travel to the stars?

Sending people to the stars will be very difficult. The distances are huge. The trip may take several generations. Families might be born who spend their whole lives on board the starship. However, the science-fiction dreams of travel (left) may one day prove to be possible. After all, it is only 380 years since Galileo first pointed a telescope to the sky.

Index

The numbers in **bold** are illustrations.

asteroid belt 13
asteroids 13, **13**
astrolabe 3, **3**
astronauts 5

Big Bang 28
black holes 27, **27**

comets 13
constellations 8–9
  Andromeda 25
  Cepheus 23
  Crux 9, **9**
  Ursa Major 8, **8**
  Ursa Minor 8, **8**
Copernicus 3

Earth 3, 4, 5, 10, **10**, 11, **11**, 12, 13, 15, **15**
  tides on 11

galaxies 24–25, 28
  elliptical 25, **25**
  irregular 25, **25**
  Milky Way 24, **24**
  spiral 25, **25**
Galilei, Galileo 3, **3**, 11, 29
gravity 11, 19, 22, 23, 27, 28

International Ultraviolet Explorer 7, **7**
InfraRed Astronomy Satellite (IRAS) 7, **7**,
  22

Jupiter **10**, 11, 14, **14**, 16, **16**
  moons of 11
  red spot 16

light-years 22, 25
Lippershey, Hans 3

Mars **10**, 11, 13, 16, **16**
  moons of 11
  surface of 16
Mercury 10, **10**, 14, **14**
  temperatures on 14
meteorites 12, **12**
meteors 12, **12**
Moon 2, 3, 11, 15
  gravity on 11
  phases of 11, **11**
moons 11
  Callisto 11
  Charon 18
  Deimos 11
  Europa 11
  Ganymede 11
  Io 11
  Phobos 11
  Titan 11

nebulae 21
  Great Nebula in Orion 21, **21**
Neptune 10, **10**, 18, **18**, 19
North Pole 8

observatories 5, 9, 19
  Kitt Peak 5
  Yerkes 5

photographs 5
planets 2, 3, 14–19, 22
Pluto 10, **10,** 11, 18, **18**
  moons of 11, 18
  temperatures on 18
pulsars 26, **26**

quasars 26, **26,** 28

radio signals 5
rockets 6

satellites 7
infrared Astronomy 7, **7,** 22
Saturn **10,** 11, 17, **18**
  moons of 11
  rings 17, **17**
Solar System 10, **10,** 13, 16, 19, 24
South Pole 9
spacecraft 17, 18, 19
  Voyager 1 17, **17**
  Voyager 2 18, **18**
space probes 19
  Pioneer 10 19, **19**
spectrometers 7
stars 2, 3, 6, 7, 8–9, **8, 9,** 13, 20, 21, 22–3, 7
  Beta Pictoris 22, **22**
  binaries 23
  clusters 22
  dwarf 20, **20**
  giants 20, **20**
  Polaris 8, **8**
  red 20, **20**
  supergiants 20
  yellow 20, **20**

starships 29, **29**
Stonehenge 2, **2**
Sun 2, 3, 7, 10, **10,** 11, **11,** 13, 14, 15, 18
sundials 3
supernovas 20, **20**

telescopes 2, 3, **3,** 4–7, 9, 19
  Hubble Space 5, **5,** 29, **29**
  Kitt Peak 5, **5**
  infrared 7
  optical 4, 5
  radio 6, 19
  ultraviolet 7
  Yerkes Observatory 5

Uranus **10,** 11, 17, **17,** 18, **18,** 19
  moons of 11
  rings 17, 18

Venus **10,** 15, **15**
  atmosphere 15
  temperatures on 15

X-ray detectors 6
X rays 6, 26

First U.S. edition 1991

Originally published by Macmillan Children's Books, a division of Macmillan Publishers, Ltd. Subsequently published by Heinemann Children's Reference, a division of Heinemann Educational Books Ltd., Halley Court, Jordan Hill, Oxford OX2 8EJ. Companies and representatives throughout the world.

CRESTWOOD·HOUSE

Macmillan Publishing Company
866 Third Avenue
New York, NY 10022

Collier Macmillan Canada, Inc.
1200 Eglinton Avenue East
Suite 200
Don Mills, Ontario M3C 3N1

Printed in Hong Kong

First Edition

10 9 8 7 6 5 4 3 2 1

Design by Julian Holland Publishing Ltd

Library of Congress Cataloging-in-Publication Data
Steele, Philip.
    Astronomy / by Philip Steele — 1st U.S. ed.
        p.   cm. — (Pocket facts)
    Includes index.
    Summary: Presents brief facts about astronomy including information about the origins of the science, the solar system. various constellations and galaxies, and other phenomena relating to outer space.
    ISBN 0-89686-586-X
    1. Astronomy — Juvenile literature. [1. Astronomy.] I. Title.
  II. Series: Pocket facts (New York, N.Y.)
QB46.S918   1991
520 — dc20

90 – 20633
CIP
AC

Acknowledgments
Illustrations: BLA Publishing Limited.
Photographs: a = above m = middle b = below
2a Science Photo Library; 2b ZEFA; 3a Michael Holford; 5a, 5b, 6a, 6b, 7b, 10a, 11b, 12a Science Photo Library; 12b John Mason; 13b, 14a Science Photo Library; 15a NASA/Science Photo Library; 15b, 16a, 16♯ 17a, 17b, 21, 22a, 22b, 24a, 26a, 26b, 29a Science Photo Library.